# Sudoku Puzzles for Children. Ages 4-8

Every child can do it.

Step by step sudoku instructions. For teaching kids sudoku at home or at school.

Visit www.sudokids.com

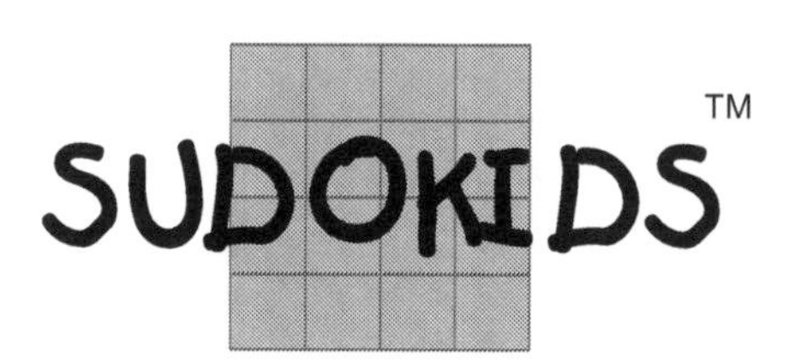


Thanks for trying our Sudoku puzzle book for children. Please look out for new titles, country specific books, teacher resources and bulk school ordering information on our website - www.sudokids.com.

Books can be customized to suit special requirements for bulk ordering.

Dedicated to my wife Lauren and children Tzvi, Shayna and Ariella. Also thanks to the top life and business coach in Africa, Daphna Horowitz.



A catalog record of this book is available from: National Library of South Africa, Pretoria

www.sudokids.com  ISBN 978-0-620-40593-5

# Contents

# Introduction to Sudoku

The first Sudoku related puzzles can be traced back to China over 3000 years ago. The first modern sudoku puzzle was created by Howard Garnes. It was published in 1979 by Dell magazines in New York and was called Number Place . It was based on a 9x9 grid, with each row and column containing the digits 1 to 9. Within the grid, there were 9 squares of 3x3 grids, also containing the numbers 1 to 9.

In the mid 1980's, the Japanese company Nikoli published the first puzzles called Sudoku, with Su meaning number and Doku meaning single. Its popularity has increased enormously, and it is now the worlds most addictive and fastest growing puzzle game.

Sudokids has been developed for children aged 4-8 who are new to Sudoku puzzles. Sudokids uses a 4x4 grid instead of the standard 9x9 grid to teach the core concepts and basic methodology of completing a Sudoku puzzle.

# Introduction for Teachers & Parents

As an untreated Sudoku addict , I spend many hours thriving in the challenge of solving complicated puzzles. Sudokus' distinct advantage over other mathematical games/puzzles is its reliance on using logical reasoning and deduction to solve numeracy puzzles, without requiring mathematical calculations.

I have developed Sudokids as a fun, challenging and stimulating educational tool inviting children into the brain domain of adults.

Sudokids is highly effective for getting children interested and involved in puzzles, problem solving and maths. Sudokids puzzles develop and stimulate the brain, teaching flexibility, creativity, concentration and raw logic to children in the school and home environment.

# Teacher and Student Assessment

On each page you will find rubrics that can be used by teachers and students to assess their work.
1. Not Achieved 2. Partially Achieved
3. Satisfactorily Achieved 4. Excellent

Teachers

Students

# School Curriculum

Sudokids has been designed around the Grades **1 - 3** school curriculum (Grade K kids can also do it) and associated teaching methods; and will equip learners with skills, knowledge and understanding in many learning areas.

Instead of focusing on a specific country's curriculum, I have broadly developed the lessons around the following learning areas, outcomes and expectations, so that they can be incorporated into classroom lessons and group activities:

**Mathematics & Numeracy:** numbers, relationships, patterns, shapes, space, data handling, probability, co-ordinates and problem solving.

**Language & Communication:** listening, speaking, reading, writing, strategy, thinking & reasoning.

**Life Skills/Orientation & Personal Development:** Thinking, evaluating, analyzing, collaboration team-work and decision making.

# Number Formatting

Sudokids uses the numbers from 1 -4 to complete a puzzle. Try drawing these numbers.

1 Number 1 - Start at the top and draw a straight line down.

2 Number 2 - Start at the top left, curve round to the bottom and then draw straight to the right.

3 Number 3 - Start at the top left, curve round to the middle and then round again from right to left.

4 Number 4 - Start at the top and draw down to the left and across to the right. Then draw another line straight down in the middle.

# Squares

All Sudoku puzzles have squares.
All Sudokids puzzles have 4 big squares.

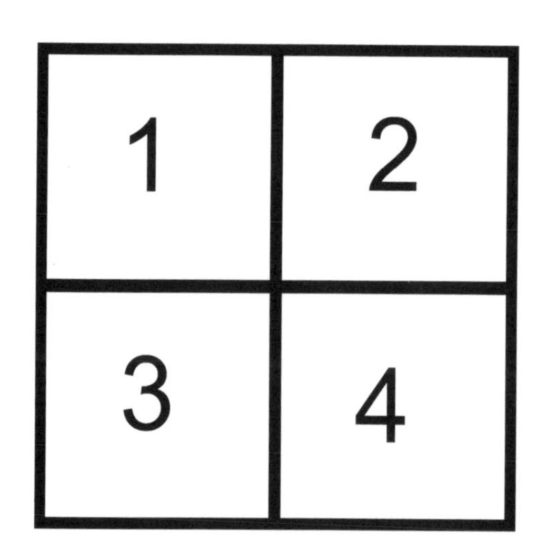

Inside each big square there are
4 little squares.

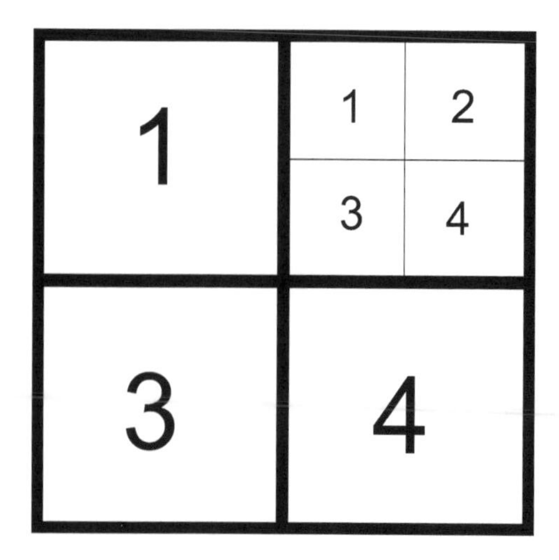


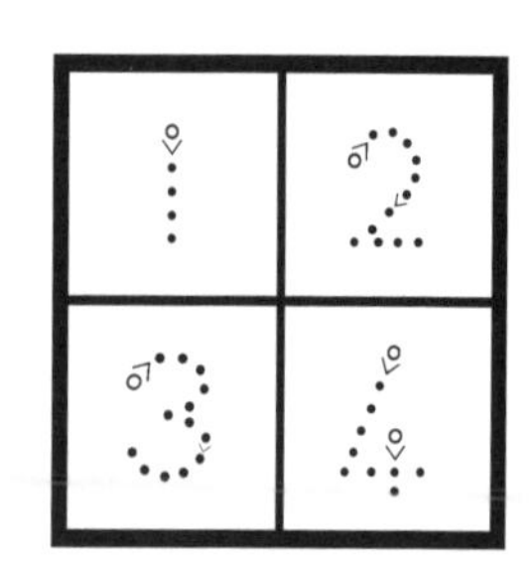

# Squares

In every big square with 4 little squares, you have to have all the numbers 1, 2, 3 and 4.

Can you write the missing numbers in the empty squares?

| 1 | 2 |
|---|---|
| 3 |   |

| 1 | 2 |
|---|---|
|   | 4 |

| 1 |   |
|---|---|
| 3 | 4 |

|   | 2 |
|---|---|
| 3 | 4 |

| 2 |   |
|---|---|
| 4 | 1 |

| 3 | 1 |
|---|---|
|   | 2 |

| 4 | 1 |
|---|---|
|   | 3 |

| 1 | 4 |
|---|---|
| 2 |   |

|   | 3 |
|---|---|
| 4 | 1 |

# Columns

Sudoku puzzles have columns going down.

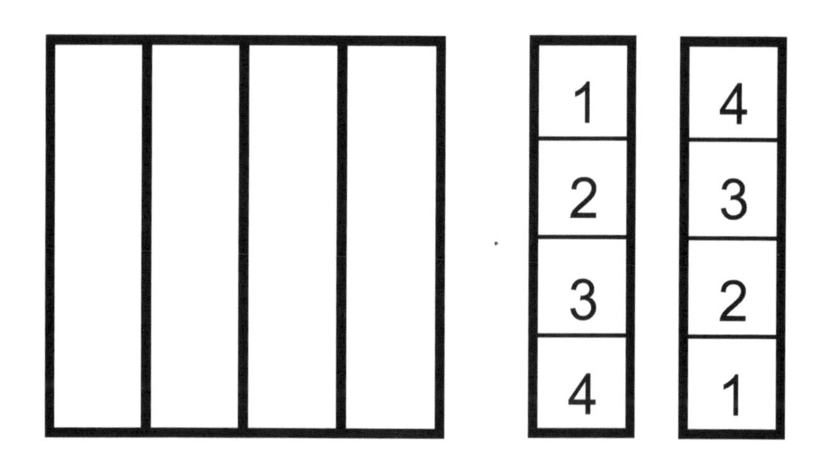


In every column in a Sudokids puzzle, you must also have the numbers **1**, **2**, **3** and **4**.

Can you fill in the missing number in each of the columns below?

| | | | | |
|---|---|---|---|---|
| 1 | 1 | 1 | 3 | 4 |
| 2 | | 4 | 2 | |
| 3 | 3 | | 1 | 3 |
| | 4 | 2 | | 2 |

# Rows

Sudoku puzzles have rows going across.

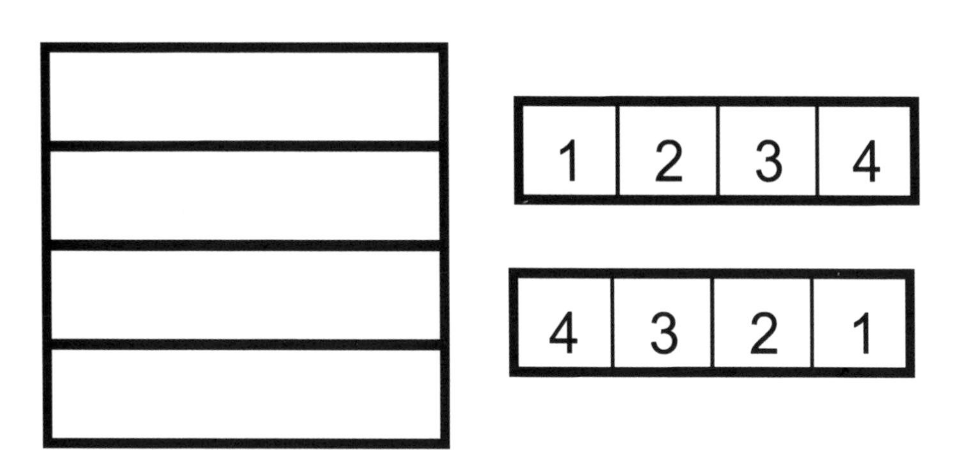


In every row in a Sudokids puzzle, you must also have the numbers 1, 2, 3 and 4.

Can you fill in the missing number in each of the rows below?

| | | | |
|---|---|---|---|
| 1 | 2 | 3 | |

| | | | |
|---|---|---|---|
| 1 | | 3 | 4 |

| | | | |
|---|---|---|---|
| 1 | 2 | | 4 |

| | | | |
|---|---|---|---|
| 1 | 2 | 3 | |

| | | | |
|---|---|---|---|
| 3 | 4 | 1 | |

| | | | |
|---|---|---|---|
| 4 | 2 | | 3 |

# L Shape

As I am sure you have noticed, the rows and columns join together. When they do join, you must make sure that there are still only the numbers 1, 2, 3, and 4 in each row and column. Good Luck !!

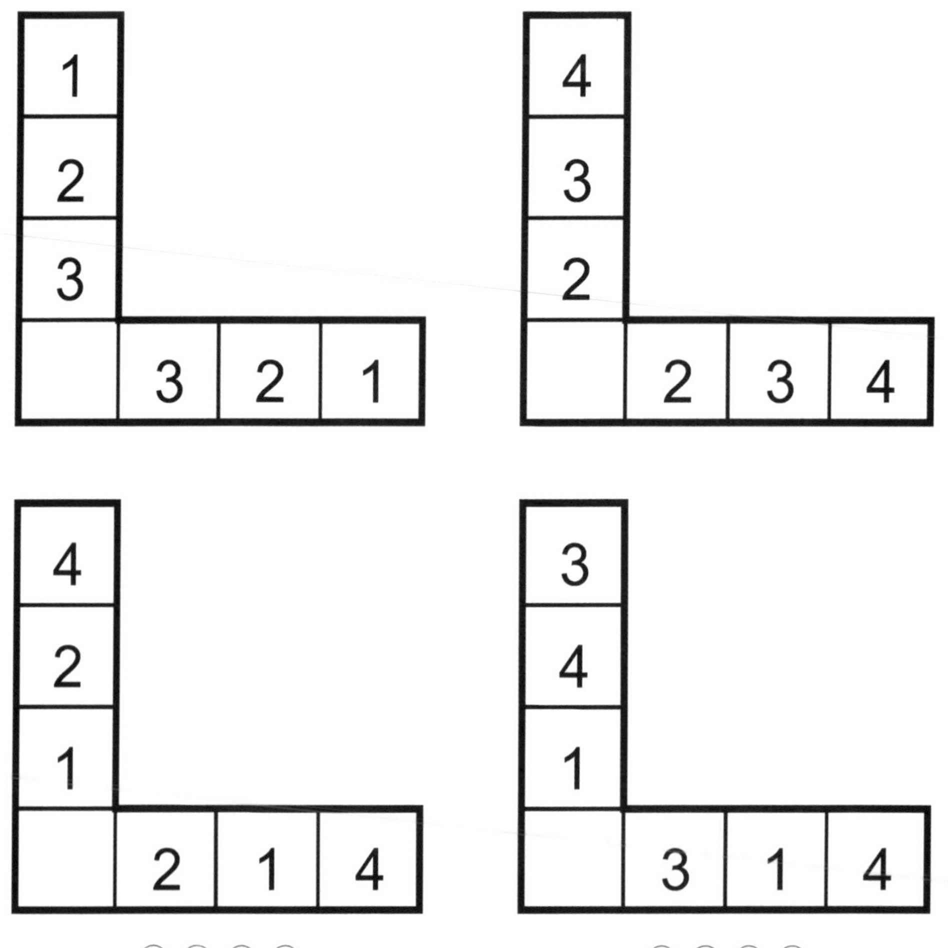

# L Shape

First do the row and then do the column.

| | | | |
|---|---|---|---|
| | 2 | 3 | 4 |
| | | | |
| 3 | | | |
| 4 | | | |

| | | | |
|---|---|---|---|
| | | | 4 |
| | | | |
| | | | 2 |
| 3 | 4 | | 1 |

| | | | |
|---|---|---|---|
| 1 | 2 | 3 | |
| | | | |
| | | | 3 |
| | | | 2 |

| | | | |
|---|---|---|---|
| | | | |
| 2 | | | |
| 3 | | | |
| | 4 | 2 | 3 |

Remember, you can not have **2** of the same numbers in a row or column. Do the corner squares first in these puzzles.

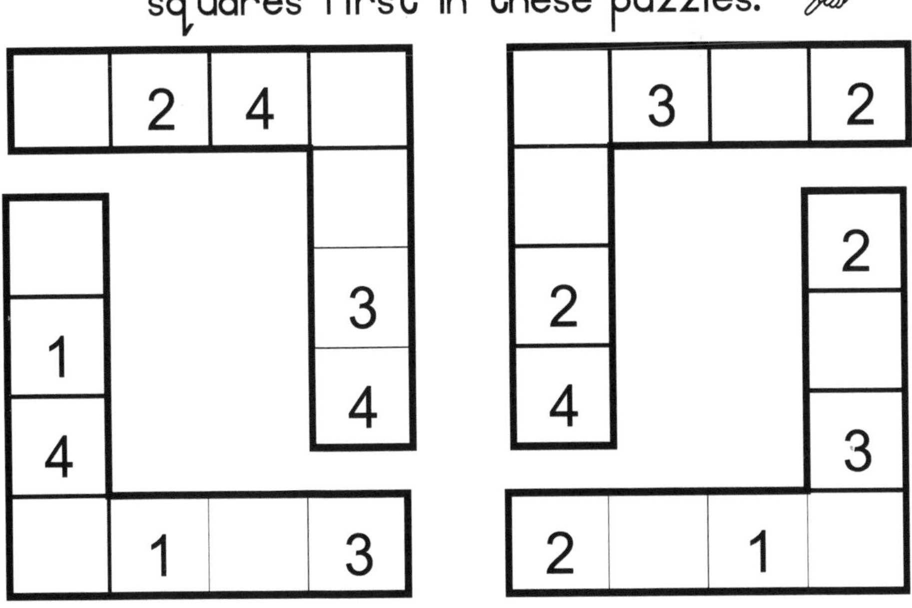

# Double Columns

Now we get to the fun part. We join 2 squares together to make 2 columns.

Remember to keep in mind the 4 different numbers for the squares and for the columns.

You can choose to try a square first and then a column. Or try a column first and then a square. It's usually easier to try the one that has more numbers in it.

Try the squares first in these puzzles.

| 1 | 2 |
|---|---|
|   | 4 |
|   | 3 |
| 4 | 1 |

| 1 | 2 |
|---|---|
|   | 3 |
|   | 4 |
| 2 | 1 |

| 1 |   |
|---|---|
| 2 | 4 |
| 3 |   |
| 4 | 1 |

|   | 1 |
|---|---|
| 3 | 2 |
| 2 | 4 |
|   | 3 |

# Double Columns

Try the columns first in these puzzles.

| | |
|---|---|
| 1 | 3 |
| 2 | 4 |
| | |
| 4 | 1 |

| | |
|---|---|
| 1 | 2 |
| 4 | 3 |
| | |
| 2 | 1 |

| | |
|---|---|
| 1 | 4 |
| 2 | |
| | 2 |
| 4 | 1 |

| | |
|---|---|
| | 1 |
| 3 | 2 |
| 2 | |
| 1 | 3 |

That was easy. Now it gets a bit more difficult. You have to choose to do either the squares or the columns first. Go for it!

| | |
|---|---|
| | 1 |
| 3 | 2 |
| 2 | |
| | 3 |

| | |
|---|---|
| 1 | 4 |
| 2 | |
| 3 | 1 |
| | |

| | |
|---|---|
| 1 | |
| 2 | 4 |
| | |
| 4 | 1 |

| | |
|---|---|
| | 1 |
| 3 | |
| 2 | 4 |
| | |

Remember, you can't have **2** of the same numbers in a big square or column.

# Double Row

Great ! Now we are going to do **2** rows. It's very similar to **2** columns. Instead of thinking up and down, you've got to think sideways.

Remember, you can't have **2** of the same numbers in a big square or in a row.

Try the big squares first.

| | | | |
|---|---|---|---|
| 1 | 3 | 4 | 2 |
| 2 | | | 1 |

| | | | |
|---|---|---|---|
| 2 | | | 3 |
| 3 | 1 | 4 | 2 |

| | | | |
|---|---|---|---|
| 2 | 4 | 1 | 3 |
| | 1 | 4 | |

| | | | |
|---|---|---|---|
| | 2 | 4 | |
| 4 | 3 | 1 | 2 |

| | | | |
|---|---|---|---|
| 1 | | | 2 |
| 2 | 4 | 3 | 1 |

| | | | |
|---|---|---|---|
| 1 | 4 | 2 | 3 |
| 2 | | | 4 |

# Double Row

Try the rows first in these puzzles.

| | | | |
|---|---|---|---|
| 3 | 1 | | 2 |
| 2 | 4 | | 1 |

| | | | |
|---|---|---|---|
| 2 | | 4 | 3 |
| 4 | | 1 | 2 |

| | | | |
|---|---|---|---|
| 2 | 4 | | 3 |
| 1 | | 4 | 2 |

| | | | |
|---|---|---|---|
| | 2 | | 3 |
| 4 | 3 | 1 | |

If you managed those puzzles, then you can easily do the ones below. No clues this time. You can choose either big squares or rows first.

| | | | |
|---|---|---|---|
| 4 | | | 3 |
| | 3 | 2 | |

| | | | |
|---|---|---|---|
| | 1 | | 2 |
| 4 | | 3 | |

| | | | |
|---|---|---|---|
| | 1 | | 3 |
| | 4 | | 2 |

| | | | |
|---|---|---|---|
| 3 | | | 4 |
| 4 | | 2 | |

# Triple Squares

Now your brain is really going to start working hard. We are going to master **3** squares. And when we put **3** squares together what do we get? You got it! You have **2** rows and also **2** columns.

Try the big squares first in these puzzles.

And remember, you must have a **1**, **2**, **3** and **4** in every row, column and square

| | | | |
|---|---|---|---|
| 1 | 4 | 2 | |
| 2 | | 1 | 4 |
| | | 3 | 1 |
| | | 4 | |

1, 2, 3, 4

| | | | |
|---|---|---|---|
| 1 | 2 | | |
| 3 | | | |
| | 3 | 2 | 1 |
| 2 | 1 | | 4 |

| | | | |
|---|---|---|---|
| | | | 1 |
| | | 3 | 2 |
| | 3 | 2 | 4 |
| 4 | 2 | 1 | |

# Squares, Squares Everywhere

When you start a puzzle, remember to try fill in the easiest square first. In puzzle A, the top left square is only missing one number. Once you fill in the correct number then the rest of the puzzle is easy. Start with the bottom right square in puzzle B.

**A**

| | | | |
|---|---|---|---|
| 1 | 3 | | 2 |
| 2 | | | 1 |
| | 1 | | |
| 4 | | | |

**B**

| | | | |
|---|---|---|---|
| 2 | | | 4 |
| 4 | | 3 | |
| | | | 3 |
| | | 2 | 1 |

**C**

| | | | |
|---|---|---|---|
| 3 | 1 | | |
| | 2 | | |
| 2 | | | 4 |
| | 4 | | 2 |

**D**

| | | | |
|---|---|---|---|
| | | 2 | 4 |
| | | | 3 |
| | 1 | | |
| 2 | | 3 | 1 |

# Columns, Rows, then Squares

We are now going to start labeling the rows and columns. The columns going down are labeled with letters (A,B,C,D). The rows going across are labeled with numbers (1, 2, 3, 4).

What numbers can you see in row 1? ______

What numbers can you see in column A? ______

What number is in row 2, column D? ______

What number is in column C, row 4? ______

In this puzzle, the grey square is in Column D and Row 1. We call it square D1.

| | A | B | C | D |
|---|---|---|---|---|
| 1 | 4 | 2 | | |
| 2 | 1 | | | 4 |
| 3 | | | | 3 |
| 4 | | | 1 | 2 |

Lets start with that column because it's the easiest. Write in the missing number in D1.

The square next to it is called C1. Write in the missing number in C1. Now each big square has only one number missing and it is easy to finish the puzzle.

# Thinking out the Square

In puzzle A, first do the top square (C1) and then do square D3. Now, you can see there are 2 numbers missing in column C i.e. 1 and 2. The 1 can go into either square, but the 2 can't go into square C4, because there's already a 2 in row 4.

So, square C3 must be a 2. Finish puzzle A and then try the others.

Easiest First

**A**

C1

| | A | B | C | D |
|---|---|---|---|---|
| 1 | | | | 2 |
| 2 | | | 3 | 1 |
| 3 | | 3 | | |
| 4 | | 2 | | 3 |

| | A | B | C | D |
|---|---|---|---|---|
| 1 | 1 | | | |
| 2 | 2 | 4 | | |
| 3 | | | | 4 |
| 4 | 4 | | 1 | |

| | A | B | C | D |
|---|---|---|---|---|
| 1 | | 4 | | 2 |
| 2 | 1 | | | 3 |
| 3 | | | 2 | |
| 4 | | | | 4 |

C2

| | A | B | C | D |
|---|---|---|---|---|
| 1 | | 2 | | 3 |
| 2 | 3 | | 4 | |
| 3 | 1 | | | |
| 4 | | 3 | | |

B2

# Triple Squares

Excellent, you are really doing great!! Lets do a few more of the triple square ones. I'll help you with the first one and you can try the rest. In puzzle A, the top big square is missing a 1 and a 4. The 4 can't go in Column D, so it must go in square C2, and the 1 must go in D1.

So, D3 must be a 2. C3 and C4 are also missing a 1 and 3. The 1 can't go in C3. It must go in C4. Now try and finish the rest of the puzzles.

**A**

| | A | B | C | D |
|---|---|---|---|---|
| 1 | | | 2 | |
| 2 | | | | 3 |
| 3 | 1 | | | |
| 4 | | 2 | | 4 |

| | A | B | C | D |
|---|---|---|---|---|
| 1 | 1 | | | |
| 2 | | 2 | | |
| 3 | | | 3 | |
| 4 | 2 | | | 4 |

| | A | B | C | D |
|---|---|---|---|---|
| 1 | | 2 | | 3 |
| 2 | 3 | | | |
| 3 | | | 1 | |
| 4 | | | | 2 |

| | A | B | C | D |
|---|---|---|---|---|
| 1 | 4 | | | 3 |
| 2 | | | 4 | |
| 3 | | 2 | | |
| 4 | 1 | | | |

# My First Full Sudokids puzzle

Lets go through a full puzzle from start to finish, using all the skills we have learnt so far. Lets start with the easiest square. Column A is only missing one number, a **3**. Now, row **3** is only missing a **2**.

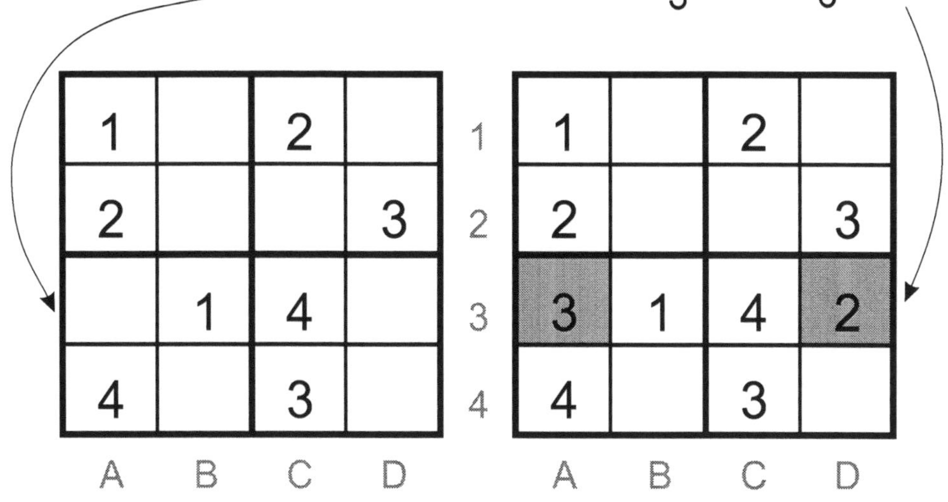


You can do B4 and D4 to finish their big squares, D1 to finish Column D and C2 to finish column C. The last two squares in Column B are now easy.

| | A | B | C | D |
|---|---|---|---|---|
| 1 | 1 | | 2 | 4 |
| 2 | 2 | | 1 | 3 |
| 3 | 3 | 1 | 4 | 2 |
| 4 | 4 | 2 | 3 | 1 |

B4 D4

| | A | B | C | D |
|---|---|---|---|---|
| 1 | 1 | 3 | 2 | 4 |
| 2 | 2 | 4 | 1 | 3 |
| 3 | 3 | 1 | 4 | 2 |
| 4 | 4 | 2 | 3 | 1 |

# My First Sudokids Puzzles

Now you are ready to complete a Sudokids puzzle on your own. You are going to finish a full puzzle with 4 squares, 4 rows and 4 columns by using the skills you have learnt.

In the puzzles below, choose the easiest row, column or square to start with and then try finish the puzzles. Good Luck !!

| | | | |
|---|---|---|---|
| 1 | 3 | | 2 |
| 2 | | | 1 |
| | 2 | 1 | 3 |
| 3 | | 2 | |

| | | | |
|---|---|---|---|
| 1 | 3 | | 2 |
| | 2 | 1 | |
| 2 | | | 4 |
| 3 | 4 | | 1 |

| | | | |
|---|---|---|---|
| | 3 | 2 | 4 |
| 4 | | | 3 |
| 3 | 1 | | |
| 2 | | 3 | 1 |

# Final Summary & Rules

That's it! You are now a Sudokids Puzzle Master.

You have learnt everything you need to know to finish all the puzzles in this book. Just keep in mind the following rules and instructions as you do each puzzle:

1. Every square, column and row must have the numbers 1, 2, 3 and 4.
2. Look at all 4 squares, all 4 rows and all 4 columns to choose where to start.
3. Choose the easiest first. Usually it's the one with the most numbers.
4. When you write a number in a small square, check the following:

There is no duplicate number in its column.
There is no duplicate number in its row.
There is no duplicate number in its big square.

## Most Important Rule

# Have lots of FUN!

Quick & Easy
Sudoku

SUDOKIDS
.com
TM

# Quick & Easy

**1**

| | | | |
|---|---|---|---|
| 2 | 3 | | 4 |
| 1 | | 2 | 3 |
| | 1 | 3 | |
| 3 | | 4 | 1 |

**2**

| | | | |
|---|---|---|---|
| 3 | 1 | | 2 |
| 4 | | 1 | |
| 2 | 4 | | 1 |
| | 3 | 2 | 4 |

**3**

| | | | |
|---|---|---|---|
| 2 | 3 | | 4 |
| | 1 | 3 | |
| 3 | 2 | | 1 |
| 1 | | 2 | 3 |

**4**

| | | | |
|---|---|---|---|
| | 1 | 2 | 4 |
| 4 | 2 | | 3 |
| | 3 | 4 | |
| 2 | | 3 | 1 |

sudokids.com

**5**

| | | | |
|---|---|---|---|
| 2 | 3 | | 4 |
| 4 | | 3 | 2 |
| | 2 | 4 | 1 |
| 1 | 4 | 2 | |

**6**

| | | | |
|---|---|---|---|
| | 1 | 3 | 4 |
| 4 | 3 | | 2 |
| | 2 | 4 | |
| 1 | | 2 | 3 |

# Quick & Easy

**7**

| | | | |
|---|---|---|---|
| 3 | 1 | | 4 |
| | 4 | 1 | 3 |
| 4 | 2 | | 1 |
| 1 | | 4 | |

**8**

| | | | |
|---|---|---|---|
| 3 | | | 2 |
| 4 | 2 | 1 | |
| 2 | | | 1 |
| | 3 | 2 | 4 |

**9**

| | | | |
|---|---|---|---|
| 1 | | 2 | 4 |
| 4 | 2 | 3 | |
| | 4 | | 2 |
| 2 | 1 | 4 | |

**10**

| | | | |
|---|---|---|---|
| | 1 | 4 | 3 |
| 4 | | | 2 |
| 1 | 2 | 3 | |
| 3 | | 2 | 1 |

**11**

| | | | |
|---|---|---|---|
| 2 | 1 | | 3 |
| 4 | | 2 | 1 |
| | 2 | 3 | 4 |
| 3 | 4 | | |

**12**

| | | | |
|---|---|---|---|
| 1 | 2 | 3 | |
| 4 | | 2 | 1 |
| | 1 | | 2 |
| 2 | 4 | | 3 |

# Quick & Easy

13

| | | | |
|---|---|---|---|
| 1 | 4 | | 3 |
| | 2 | 4 | 1 |
| | 1 | 3 | |
| 2 | | 1 | 4 |

14

| | | | |
|---|---|---|---|
| 4 | 3 | 2 | |
| 1 | | 3 | 4 |
| | 1 | | 3 |
| | 4 | 1 | 2 |

15

| | | | |
|---|---|---|---|
| 2 | 1 | | 4 |
| 4 | | 2 | 1 |
| | 4 | 1 | |
| 1 | 2 | | 3 |

16

| | | | |
|---|---|---|---|
| 4 | 1 | 3 | |
| 2 | | 1 | 4 |
| | 4 | | 3 |
| 3 | | 4 | 1 |

17

| | | | |
|---|---|---|---|
| 4 | | 2 | 1 |
| 2 | 1 | 3 | |
| | 4 | | 2 |
| 1 | | 4 | 3 |

18

| | | | |
|---|---|---|---|
| | 1 | 3 | |
| 4 | 3 | | 2 |
| 3 | | 4 | 1 |
| | 4 | 2 | |

# Quick & Easy

19

| | | | |
|---|---|---|---|
| | 2 | 4 | |
| 3 | | | 1 |
| 4 | | 3 | 2 |
| | 3 | 1 | |

20

| | | | |
|---|---|---|---|
| | 1 | 2 | 3 |
| 2 | | | 4 |
| 1 | 4 | 3 | |
| | | 4 | 1 |

21

| | | | |
|---|---|---|---|
| 4 | 2 | | 1 |
| 3 | | 2 | |
| 1 | | | 2 |
| | 4 | 1 | 3 |

22

| | | | |
|---|---|---|---|
| 1 | | 4 | 3 |
| 4 | 3 | | |
| | 1 | 2 | |
| 2 | | 3 | 1 |



23

| | | | |
|---|---|---|---|
| 3 | | | 2 |
| | 2 | 1 | 3 |
| 2 | | 3 | 1 |
| | 3 | 2 | |

24

| | | | |
|---|---|---|---|
| | 4 | | 3 |
| 3 | 2 | | 1 |
| | 1 | 3 | 2 |
| 2 | | 1 | |

# Quick & Easy

25

| | | | |
|---|---|---|---|
| 3 | 1 | | |
| 4 | | 3 | 1 |
| | 4 | 1 | |
| 1 | 3 | | 2 |

26

| | | | |
|---|---|---|---|
| | 1 | | 4 |
| 3 | | 2 | 1 |
| | 3 | 1 | |
| 1 | | 4 | 3 |

27

| | | | |
|---|---|---|---|
| | 2 | 3 | |
| 4 | 3 | 2 | 1 |
| | 1 | 4 | |
| 2 | | | 3 |

SUDOKIDS .com

28

| | | | |
|---|---|---|---|
| 4 | | 2 | 1 |
| 2 | 1 | 3 | |
| | 4 | | 2 |
| 1 | | 4 | 3 |

29

| | | | |
|---|---|---|---|
| 3 | 2 | 1 | |
| 4 | | 2 | 3 |
| | 4 | | 2 |
| 2 | | | 1 |

30

| | | | |
|---|---|---|---|
| 1 | 2 | 3 | |
| | 3 | 2 | 1 |
| | 4 | | 2 |
| | | 4 | |

# Quick & Easy

**31**

| | | | |
|---|---|---|---|
| | 4 | 3 | |
| 3 | 1 | | 4 |
| | | 1 | 3 |
| | 3 | 4 | |

**32**

| | | | |
|---|---|---|---|
| 1 | | 4 | |
| 2 | 4 | 3 | |
| | 2 | 1 | |
| 4 | | | 3 |

**33**

| | | | |
|---|---|---|---|
| | 1 | 2 | |
| 4 | 2 | | 1 |
| 1 | | 4 | |
| | 4 | | 3 |

**34**

| | | | |
|---|---|---|---|
| | 3 | 2 | 1 |
| 1 | | | 4 |
| | 1 | | 3 |
| | 4 | 1 | |

**35**

| | | | |
|---|---|---|---|
| | 1 | 3 | |
| 2 | | 1 | |
| | 4 | | 3 |
| 3 | | 4 | 1 |

**36**

| | | | |
|---|---|---|---|
| | | 2 | 4 |
| | 2 | 3 | |
| | 4 | | 2 |
| | 1 | 4 | 3 |

Medium
Sudoku

SUDOKIDS
.com
TM

# Medium

37

| | | | |
|---|---|---|---|
| | 2 | | 4 |
| 3 | | | 2 |
| | 3 | | |
| 2 | | 4 | 3 |

38

| | | | |
|---|---|---|---|
| | 4 | 3 | |
| 3 | 1 | | |
| | | 1 | 3 |
| | 3 | 4 | |

39

| | | | |
|---|---|---|---|
| 3 | | | 2 |
| | 2 | 3 | |
| | 4 | 2 | |
| 2 | | | 4 |

40

| | | | |
|---|---|---|---|
| 1 | | | 3 |
| | 2 | 4 | |
| | 1 | 3 | |
| 2 | | | 4 |

41

| | | | |
|---|---|---|---|
| | 1 | | 3 |
| 4 | | 2 | |
| | 2 | | 4 |
| 1 | | 3 | |

42

| | | | |
|---|---|---|---|
| 2 | | 4 | |
| | 1 | | 3 |
| 1 | | 3 | |
| | 2 | | 4 |

# Medium

**43**

|   |   |   |   |
|---|---|---|---|
|   | 4 |   | 1 |
| 3 |   | 2 |   |
|   | 3 |   | 2 |
| 1 |   | 4 |   |

**44**

|   |   |   |   |
|---|---|---|---|
| 1 |   |   | 3 |
| 2 |   |   | 4 |
|   | 1 | 3 |   |
|   | 2 | 4 |   |

**45**

|   |   |   |   |
|---|---|---|---|
| 4 |   | 1 |   |
|   | 1 |   | 4 |
| 2 |   | 3 |   |
|   | 3 |   | 2 |

**46**

|   |   |   |   |
|---|---|---|---|
|   | 3 | 2 |   |
|   | 1 | 4 |   |
|   | 2 | 3 |   |
| 3 |   |   | 2 |

**47**

|   |   |   |   |
|---|---|---|---|
| 1 |   |   | 3 |
|   | 2 | 4 |   |
|   | 1 | 3 |   |
| 2 |   |   | 4 |

**48**

|   |   |   |   |
|---|---|---|---|
| 4 |   | 2 |   |
|   |   | 3 | 4 |
|   | 1 |   | 3 |
|   | 4 | 1 |   |

# Medium

**49**

| | | | |
|---|---|---|---|
| 4 | | | 1 |
| 2 | | 3 | |
| | 4 | | 2 |
| | 2 | | 3 |

**50**

| | | | |
|---|---|---|---|
| | 3 | 4 | |
| 2 | | | 3 |
| 4 | | | 1 |
| | 1 | 2 | |

**51**

| | | | |
|---|---|---|---|
| | 1 | 2 | |
| | 2 | | 1 |
| 1 | | 4 | |
| | 4 | | 3 |



**52**

| | | | |
|---|---|---|---|
| | 3 | 2 | |
| 1 | | | 4 |
| 2 | | | 3 |
| | 4 | | 2 |

**53**

| | | | |
|---|---|---|---|
| | 2 | 4 | |
| 3 | | | 1 |
| 4 | | | 2 |
| | 3 | 1 | |

**54**

| | | | |
|---|---|---|---|
| | 1 | 2 | 3 |
| 2 | | | 4 |
| 1 | | 3 | |
| | | | 1 |

# Medium

**55**

| | | | |
|---|---|---|---|
| | 1 | 3 | |
| 2 | | 1 | |
| | 4 | 2 | |
| | 2 | | 1 |

**56**

| | | | |
|---|---|---|---|
| | | 2 | |
| 1 | 2 | 3 | |
| | 4 | | 2 |
| | 1 | | 3 |

**57**

| | | | |
|---|---|---|---|
| | 2 | | 4 |
| 4 | | 2 | |
| | 1 | | |
| 2 | | | 3 |

**58**

| | | | |
|---|---|---|---|
| | 3 | 2 | |
| | 1 | | |
| | | 4 | |
| 3 | | 1 | 2 |

**59**

| | | | |
|---|---|---|---|
| | 3 | | 4 |
| | | | 2 |
| | | 4 | 1 |
| 1 | 4 | | |

**60**

| | | | |
|---|---|---|---|
| | 1 | 2 | 4 |
| 4 | | | 3 |
| | 3 | | |
| 2 | | | |

# Medium

61

| | | | |
|---|---|---|---|
| 1 | | | 2 |
| | | 1 | |
| | 4 | 3 | |
| 3 | | | 4 |

62

| | | | |
|---|---|---|---|
| | 1 | 2 | |
| 2 | | | 3 |
| 4 | | | 1 |
| | 3 | | |

63

| | | | |
|---|---|---|---|
| 1 | | 4 | |
| 2 | 4 | 3 | |
| | 2 | 1 | |
| 4 | | | 3 |

64

| | | | |
|---|---|---|---|
| 4 | | 1 | |
| | 1 | 3 | |
| | 2 | | 1 |
| | | | 3 |

65

| | | | |
|---|---|---|---|
| 1 | | 2 | 4 |
| 4 | 2 | 3 | |
| | 4 | | 2 |
| 2 | 1 | 4 | |

66

| | | | |
|---|---|---|---|
| | 4 | | 3 |
| | | | 1 |
| | 1 | 3 | |
| 4 | | 1 | |

# Medium

**67**

| | | | |
|---|---|---|---|
| | 1 | | |
| 4 | | 3 | 1 |
| | 4 | 1 | |
| 1 | | | 2 |

**68**

| | | | |
|---|---|---|---|
| | 2 | | 4 |
| | | 2 | |
| 4 | 1 | 3 | |
| | | | 1 |

**69**

| | | | |
|---|---|---|---|
| | 1 | 3 | |
| 2 | | | |
| 3 | | | 1 |
| | 4 | 2 | |

**70**

| | | | |
|---|---|---|---|
| | 2 | | 3 |
| 3 | | 2 | |
| | 1 | | |
| 4 | | 1 | |

SUDOKIDS.com

**71**

| | | | |
|---|---|---|---|
| | | | 4 |
| | | 3 | 1 |
| | 3 | 1 | |
| 1 | 2 | | |

**72**

| | | | |
|---|---|---|---|
| | | 3 | 2 |
| | | 1 | 4 |
| 1 | 4 | | |
| | 2 | | |

Challenging
Sudoku

SUDOKIDS
.com
TM

# Challenging

**73**

| | | | |
|---|---|---|---|
| | 1 | | 4 |
| 4 | | | 3 |
| | 3 | | |
| 2 | | | |

**74**

| | | | |
|---|---|---|---|
| | | 2 | 4 |
| 4 | 2 | | |
| 1 | | | 2 |
| | | 4 | |

**75**

| | | | |
|---|---|---|---|
| 4 | | 3 | |
| | | | |
| 3 | | | 1 |
| | 4 | 2 | |

SUDOKIDS .com

**76**

| | | | |
|---|---|---|---|
| 1 | | | 3 |
| | 2 | | |
| | | 1 | |
| 2 | | | 4 |

**77**

| | | | |
|---|---|---|---|
| | | 2 | |
| | 2 | 3 | |
| 4 | | 1 | |
| | 1 | | |

**78**

| | | | |
|---|---|---|---|
| | 2 | 4 | |
| 3 | | | 1 |
| | | | 2 |
| | | 1 | |

# Challenging

**79**

| | | | |
|---|---|---|---|
| | 4 | | 1 |
| 2 | | 3 | |
| | | | 3 |
| 1 | | 4 | |

**80**

| | | | |
|---|---|---|---|
| 1 | 2 | | 3 |
| | | | |
| | 3 | | 1 |
| 2 | | | |

**81**

| | | | |
|---|---|---|---|
| 4 | | 1 | |
| | 1 | | 4 |
| 3 | | 2 | |
| | 2 | | |

**82**

| | | | |
|---|---|---|---|
| | 2 | | 1 |
| | 3 | | 4 |
| 2 | | | 3 |
| | | 1 | |

**83**

| | | | |
|---|---|---|---|
| 1 | | | 3 |
| | 2 | 4 | |
| | 1 | | |
| 2 | | | 4 |

**84**

| | | | |
|---|---|---|---|
| 3 | | | 4 |
| | 1 | 2 | |
| | 3 | 4 | |
| | | | 2 |

# Challenging

85

| | | | |
|---|---|---|---|
| 4 | | | |
| | 1 | 3 | |
| | | | 2 |
| | 2 | | 3 |

86

| | | | |
|---|---|---|---|
| 4 | | | 3 |
| | 3 | 2 | |
| 3 | | 4 | |
| | | | 1 |

87

| | | | |
|---|---|---|---|
| 2 | | 4 | |
| | | 3 | |
| | 1 | | 3 |
| | 2 | 1 | |

88

| | | | |
|---|---|---|---|
| | 1 | 3 | |
| | 2 | 4 | |
| 2 | 3 | 1 | |
| | | | |

SUDOKIDS.com

89

| | | | |
|---|---|---|---|
| | 2 | | 1 |
| 3 | | 2 | |
| | | | 2 |
| | 4 | 1 | |

90

| | | | |
|---|---|---|---|
| | 1 | | 2 |
| 3 | | | 4 |
| 1 | | 2 | |
| | | | 1 |

# Challenging

**91**

| | | | |
|---|---|---|---|
| 4 | | | 3 |
| 2 | | | |
| | 4 | | 2 |
| | | 1 | |

**92**

| | | | |
|---|---|---|---|
| | | | 1 |
| | | 2 | |
| | 2 | | 4 |
| 3 | | | |

**93**

| | | | |
|---|---|---|---|
| | 2 | | 1 |
| | | 4 | |
| 1 | 3 | | |
| | | | |

**94**

| | | | |
|---|---|---|---|
| 3 | | | |
| | 2 | 3 | |
| | | 1 | |
| | | | 4 |

**95**

| | | | |
|---|---|---|---|
| 2 | 4 | | |
| | | | 4 |
| | 3 | | |
| | | 3 | |

**96**

| | | | |
|---|---|---|---|
| 3 | | | |
| | 4 | | 2 |
| 2 | | | 1 |
| | | | |

SUDOKIDS.com

# Challenging

**97**

| | | | |
|---|---|---|---|
| 2 | 1 | | |
| | 3 | | |
| | | 3 | |
| | | 1 | 2 |

**98**

| | | | |
|---|---|---|---|
| 4 | | | |
| | 1 | | |
| 2 | | 4 | |
| | | 3 | |

**99**

| | | | |
|---|---|---|---|
| 4 | | | |
| | 3 | | 1 |
| | 2 | | |
| 1 | | | 3 |

**100**

| | | | |
|---|---|---|---|
| | | | 1 |
| 1 | | 2 | |
| 3 | | | 4 |
| | | | 2 |

**101**

| | | | |
|---|---|---|---|
| 4 | | | |
| | 2 | | 1 |
| | | 2 | |
| | 3 | | 4 |

**102**

| | | | |
|---|---|---|---|
| 3 | 2 | | |
| | | | 2 |
| | 4 | | |
| | | 4 | |

# Challenging

**103**

| | | | |
|---|---|---|---|
| 2 | 1 | | |
| | | | 1 |
| | 3 | | |
| | | 3 | |

**104**

| | | | |
|---|---|---|---|
| | 2 | | |
| 3 | | | |
| | 4 | 3 | |
| | | | 1 |

**105**

| | | | |
|---|---|---|---|
| 1 | | 4 | |
| | 2 | | |
| | | 3 | |
| | | | 4 |

**106**

| | | | |
|---|---|---|---|
| 3 | | | |
| | 4 | | 2 |
| 2 | | | 1 |
| | | | |

**107**

| | | | |
|---|---|---|---|
| 3 | | | 4 |
| | | 2 | |
| 4 | | | |
| | 3 | | 1 |

**108**

| | | | |
|---|---|---|---|
| | 2 | | |
| | | 3 | 2 |
| | 4 | | |
| | | | 1 |

Solutions

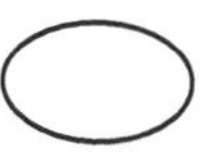

SUDOKIDS
TM
.com

# Quick & Easy

Page 26

**1**

| 2 | 3 | 1 | 4 |
|---|---|---|---|
| 1 | 4 | 2 | 3 |
| 4 | 1 | 3 | 2 |
| 3 | 2 | 4 | 1 |

**2**

| 3 | 1 | 4 | 2 |
|---|---|---|---|
| 4 | 2 | 1 | 3 |
| 2 | 4 | 3 | 1 |
| 1 | 3 | 2 | 4 |

**3**

| 2 | 3 | 1 | 4 |
|---|---|---|---|
| 4 | 1 | 3 | 2 |
| 3 | 2 | 4 | 1 |
| 1 | 4 | 2 | 3 |

**4**

| 3 | 1 | 2 | 4 |
|---|---|---|---|
| 4 | 2 | 1 | 3 |
| 1 | 3 | 4 | 2 |
| 2 | 4 | 3 | 1 |

**5**

| 2 | 3 | 1 | 4 |
|---|---|---|---|
| 4 | 1 | 3 | 2 |
| 3 | 2 | 4 | 1 |
| 1 | 4 | 2 | 3 |

**6**

| 2 | 1 | 3 | 4 |
|---|---|---|---|
| 4 | 3 | 1 | 2 |
| 3 | 2 | 4 | 1 |
| 1 | 4 | 2 | 3 |

Page 27

**7**

| 3 | 1 | 2 | 4 |
|---|---|---|---|
| 2 | 4 | 1 | 3 |
| 4 | 2 | 3 | 1 |
| 1 | 3 | 4 | 2 |

**8**

| 3 | 1 | 4 | 2 |
|---|---|---|---|
| 4 | 2 | 1 | 3 |
| 2 | | | 1 |
| | 3 | 2 | 4 |

**9**

| 1 | 3 | 2 | 4 |
|---|---|---|---|
| 4 | 2 | 3 | 1 |
| 3 | 4 | 1 | 2 |
| 2 | 1 | 4 | 3 |

**10**

| 2 | 1 | 4 | 3 |
|---|---|---|---|
| 4 | 3 | 1 | 2 |
| 1 | 2 | 3 | 4 |
| 3 | 4 | 2 | 1 |

**11**

| 2 | 1 | 4 | 3 |
|---|---|---|---|
| 4 | 3 | 2 | 1 |
| 1 | 2 | 3 | 4 |
| 3 | 4 | 1 | 2 |

**12**

| 1 | 2 | 3 | 4 |
|---|---|---|---|
| 4 | 3 | 2 | 1 |
| 3 | 1 | 4 | 2 |
| 2 | 4 | 1 | 3 |

# Quick & Easy

Page 28

**13**

| 1 | 4 | 2 | 3 |
|---|---|---|---|
| 3 | 2 | 4 | 1 |
| 4 | 1 | 3 | 2 |
| 2 | 3 | 1 | 4 |

**14**

| 4 | 3 | 2 | 1 |
|---|---|---|---|
| 1 | 2 | 3 | 4 |
| 4 | 1 | 2 | 3 |
| 3 | 4 | 1 | 2 |

**15**

| 2 | 1 | 3 | 4 |
|---|---|---|---|
| 4 | 3 | 2 | 1 |
| 3 | 4 | 1 | 2 |
| 1 | 2 | 4 | 3 |

**16**

| 4 | 1 | 3 | 2 |
|---|---|---|---|
| 2 | 3 | 1 | 4 |
| 1 | 4 | 2 | 3 |
| 3 | 2 | 4 | 1 |

**17**

| 4 | 3 | 2 | 1 |
|---|---|---|---|
| 2 | 1 | 3 | 4 |
| 3 | 4 | 1 | 2 |
| 1 | 2 | 4 | 3 |

**18**

| 2 | 1 | 3 | 4 |
|---|---|---|---|
| 4 | 3 | 1 | 2 |
| 3 | 2 | 4 | 1 |
| 1 | 4 | 2 | 3 |

Page 29

**19**

| 1 | 2 | 4 | 3 |
|---|---|---|---|
| 3 | 4 | 2 | 1 |
| 4 | 1 | 3 | 2 |
| 2 | 3 | 1 | 4 |

**20**

| 4 | 1 | 2 | 3 |
|---|---|---|---|
| 2 | 3 | 1 | 4 |
| 1 | 4 | 3 | 2 |
| 3 | 2 | 4 | 1 |

**21**

| 4 | 2 | 3 | 1 |
|---|---|---|---|
| 3 | 1 | 2 | 4 |
| 1 | 3 | 4 | 2 |
| 2 | 4 | 1 | 3 |

**22**

| 1 | 2 | 4 | 3 |
|---|---|---|---|
| 4 | 3 | 1 | 2 |
| 3 | 1 | 2 | 4 |
| 2 | 4 | 3 | 1 |

**23**

| 3 | 1 | 4 | 2 |
|---|---|---|---|
| 4 | 2 | 1 | 3 |
| 2 | 4 | 3 | 1 |
| 1 | 3 | 2 | 4 |

**24**

| 1 | 4 | 2 | 3 |
|---|---|---|---|
| 3 | 2 | 4 | 1 |
| 4 | 1 | 3 | 2 |
| 2 | 3 | 1 | 4 |

# Quick & Easy

Page 30

**25**

| 3 | 1 | 2 | 4 |
|---|---|---|---|
| 4 | 2 | 3 | 1 |
| 2 | 4 | 1 | 3 |
| 1 | 3 | 4 | 2 |

**26**

| 2 | 1 | 3 | 4 |
|---|---|---|---|
| 3 | 4 | 2 | 1 |
| 4 | 3 | 1 | 2 |
| 1 | 2 | 4 | 3 |

**27**

| 1 | 2 | 3 | 4 |
|---|---|---|---|
| 4 | 3 | 2 | 1 |
| 3 | 1 | 4 | 2 |
| 2 | 4 | 1 | 3 |

**28**

| 4 | 3 | 2 | 1 |
|---|---|---|---|
| 2 | 1 | 3 | 4 |
| 3 | 4 | 1 | 2 |
| 1 | 2 | 4 | 3 |

**29**

| 3 | 2 | 1 | 4 |
|---|---|---|---|
| 4 | 1 | 2 | 3 |
| 1 | 4 | 3 | 2 |
| 2 | 3 | 4 | 1 |

**30**

| 1 | 2 | 3 | 4 |
|---|---|---|---|
| 4 | 3 | 2 | 1 |
| 3 | 4 | 1 | 2 |
| 2 | 1 | 4 | 3 |

Page 31

**31**

| 2 | 4 | 3 | 1 |
|---|---|---|---|
| 3 | 1 | 2 | 4 |
| 4 | 2 | 1 | 3 |
| 1 | 3 | 4 | 2 |

**32**

| 1 | 3 | 4 | 2 |
|---|---|---|---|
| 2 | 4 | 3 | 1 |
| 3 | 2 | 1 | 4 |
| 4 | 1 | 2 | 3 |

**33**

| 3 | 1 | 2 | 4 |
|---|---|---|---|
| 4 | 2 | 3 | 1 |
| 1 | 3 | 4 | 2 |
| 2 | 4 | 1 | 3 |

**34**

| 4 | 3 | 2 | 1 |
|---|---|---|---|
| 1 | 2 | 3 | 4 |
| 2 | 1 | 4 | 3 |
| 3 | 4 | 1 | 2 |

**35**

| 4 | 1 | 3 | 2 |
|---|---|---|---|
| 2 | 3 | 1 | 4 |
| 1 | 4 | 2 | 3 |
| 3 | 2 | 4 | 1 |

**36**

| 1 | 3 | 2 | 4 |
|---|---|---|---|
| 4 | 2 | 3 | 1 |
| 3 | 4 | 1 | 2 |
| 2 | 1 | 4 | 3 |

# Medium

Page 33

**37**

| 1 | 2 | 3 | 4 |
|---|---|---|---|
| 3 | 4 | 1 | 2 |
| 4 | 3 | 2 | 1 |
| 2 | 1 | 4 | 3 |

**38**

| 2 | 4 | 3 | 1 |
|---|---|---|---|
| 3 | 1 | 2 | 4 |
| 4 | 2 | 1 | 3 |
| 1 | 3 | 4 | 2 |

**39**

| 3 | 1 | 4 | 2 |
|---|---|---|---|
| 4 | 2 | 3 | 1 |
| 1 | 4 | 2 | 3 |
| 2 | 3 | 1 | 4 |

**40**

| 1 | 4 | 2 | 3 |
|---|---|---|---|
| 3 | 2 | 4 | 1 |
| 4 | 1 | 3 | 2 |
| 2 | 3 | 1 | 4 |

**41**

| 2 | 1 | 4 | 3 |
|---|---|---|---|
| 4 | 3 | 2 | 1 |
| 3 | 2 | 1 | 4 |
| 1 | 4 | 3 | 2 |

**42**

| 2 | 3 | 4 | 1 |
|---|---|---|---|
| 4 | 1 | 2 | 3 |
| 1 | 4 | 3 | 2 |
| 3 | 2 | 1 | 4 |

Page 34

**43**

| 2 | 4 | 3 | 1 |
|---|---|---|---|
| 3 | 1 | 2 | 4 |
| 4 | 3 | 1 | 2 |
| 1 | 2 | 4 | 3 |

**44**

| 1 | 4 | 2 | 3 |
|---|---|---|---|
| 2 | 3 | 1 | 4 |
| 4 | 1 | 3 | 2 |
| 3 | 2 | 4 | 1 |

**45**

| 4 | 2 | 1 | 3 |
|---|---|---|---|
| 3 | 1 | 2 | 4 |
| 2 | 4 | 3 | 1 |
| 1 | 3 | 4 | 2 |

**46**

| 4 | 3 | 2 | 1 |
|---|---|---|---|
| 2 | 1 | 4 | 3 |
| 1 | 2 | 3 | 4 |
| 3 | 4 | 1 | 2 |

**47**

| 1 | 4 | 2 | 3 |
|---|---|---|---|
| 3 | 2 | 4 | 1 |
| 4 | 1 | 3 | 2 |
| 2 | 3 | 1 | 4 |

**48**

| 4 | 3 | 2 | 1 |
|---|---|---|---|
| 1 | 2 | 3 | 4 |
| 2 | 1 | 4 | 3 |
| 3 | 4 | 1 | 2 |

# Medium

Page 35

**49**

| 4 | 3 | 2 | 1 |
|---|---|---|---|
| 2 | 1 | 3 | 4 |
| 3 | 4 | 1 | 2 |
| 1 | 2 | 4 | 3 |

**50**

| 1 | 3 | 4 | 2 |
|---|---|---|---|
| 2 | 4 | 1 | 3 |
| 4 | 2 | 3 | 1 |
| 3 | 1 | 2 | 4 |

**51**

| 3 | 1 | 2 | 4 |
|---|---|---|---|
| 4 | 2 | 3 | 1 |
| 1 | 3 | 4 | 2 |
| 2 | 4 | 1 | 3 |

**52**

| 4 | 3 | 2 | 1 |
|---|---|---|---|
| 1 | 2 | 3 | 4 |
| 2 | 1 | 4 | 3 |
| 3 | 4 | 1 | 2 |

**53**

| 1 | 2 | 4 | 3 |
|---|---|---|---|
| 3 | 4 | 2 | 1 |
| 4 | 1 | 3 | 2 |
| 2 | 3 | 1 | 4 |

**54**

| 4 | 1 | 2 | 3 |
|---|---|---|---|
| 2 | 3 | 1 | 4 |
| 1 | 4 | 3 | 2 |
| 3 | 2 | 4 | 1 |

Page 36

**55**

| 4 | 1 | 3 | 2 |
|---|---|---|---|
| 2 | 3 | 1 | 4 |
| 1 | 4 | 2 | 3 |
| 3 | 2 | 4 | 1 |

**56**

| 4 | 3 | 2 | 1 |
|---|---|---|---|
| 1 | 2 | 3 | 4 |
| 3 | 4 | 1 | 2 |
| 2 | 1 | 4 | 3 |

**57**

| 1 | 2 | 3 | 4 |
|---|---|---|---|
| 4 | 3 | 2 | 1 |
| 3 | 1 | 4 | 2 |
| 2 | 4 | 1 | 3 |

**58**

| 4 | 3 | 2 | 1 |
|---|---|---|---|
| 2 | 1 | 3 | 4 |
| 1 | 2 | 4 | 3 |
| 3 | 4 | 1 | 2 |

**59**

| 2 | 3 | 1 | 4 |
|---|---|---|---|
| 4 | 1 | 3 | 2 |
| 3 | 2 | 4 | 1 |
| 1 | 4 | 2 | 3 |

**60**

| 3 | 1 | 2 | 4 |
|---|---|---|---|
| 4 | 2 | 1 | 3 |
| 1 | 3 | 4 | 2 |
| 2 | 4 | 3 | 1 |

# Medium

Page 37

**61**

| 1 | 3 | 4 | 2 |
|---|---|---|---|
| 4 | 2 | 1 | 3 |
| 2 | 4 | 3 | 1 |
| 3 | 1 | 2 | 4 |

**62**

| 3 | 1 | 2 | 4 |
|---|---|---|---|
| 2 | 4 | 1 | 3 |
| 4 | 2 | 3 | 1 |
| 1 | 3 | 4 | 2 |

**63**

| 1 | 3 | 4 | 2 |
|---|---|---|---|
| 2 | 4 | 3 | 1 |
| 3 | 2 | 1 | 4 |
| 4 | 1 | 2 | 3 |

**64**

| 4 | 3 | 1 | 2 |
|---|---|---|---|
| 2 | 1 | 3 | 4 |
| 3 | 2 | 4 | 1 |
| 1 | 4 | 2 | 3 |

**65**

| 1 | 3 | 2 | 4 |
|---|---|---|---|
| 4 | 2 | 3 | 1 |
| 3 | 4 | 1 | 2 |
| 2 | 1 | 4 | 3 |

**66**

| 1 | 4 | 2 | 3 |
|---|---|---|---|
| 3 | 2 | 4 | 1 |
| 2 | 1 | 3 | 4 |
| 4 | 3 | 1 | 2 |

Page 38

**67**

| 3 | 1 | 2 | 4 |
|---|---|---|---|
| 4 | 2 | 3 | 1 |
| 2 | 4 | 1 | 3 |
| 1 | 3 | 4 | 2 |

**68**

| 3 | 2 | 1 | 4 |
|---|---|---|---|
| 1 | 4 | 2 | 3 |
| 4 | 1 | 3 | 2 |
| 2 | 3 | 4 | 1 |

**69**

| 4 | 1 | 3 | 2 |
|---|---|---|---|
| 2 | 3 | 1 | 4 |
| 3 | 2 | 4 | 1 |
| 1 | 4 | 2 | 3 |

**70**

| 1 | 2 | 4 | 3 |
|---|---|---|---|
| 3 | 4 | 2 | 1 |
| 2 | 1 | 3 | 4 |
| 4 | 3 | 1 | 2 |

**71**

| 3 | 1 | 2 | 4 |
|---|---|---|---|
| 2 | 4 | 3 | 1 |
| 4 | 3 | 1 | 2 |
| 1 | 2 | 4 | 3 |

**72**

| 4 | 1 | 3 | 2 |
|---|---|---|---|
| 2 | 3 | 1 | 4 |
| 1 | 4 | 2 | 3 |
| 3 | 2 | 4 | 1 |

# Challenging

Page 40

**73**

| 3 | 1 | 2 | 4 |
|---|---|---|---|
| 4 | 2 | 1 | 3 |
| 1 | 3 | 4 | 2 |
| 2 | 4 | 3 | 1 |

**74**

| 3 | 1 | 2 | 4 |
|---|---|---|---|
| 4 | 2 | 1 | 3 |
| 1 | 4 | 3 | 2 |
| 2 | 3 | 4 | 1 |

**75**

| 4 | 1 | 3 | 2 |
|---|---|---|---|
| 2 | 3 | 1 | 4 |
| 3 | 2 | 4 | 1 |
| 1 | 4 | 2 | 3 |

**76**

| 1 | 4 | 2 | 3 |
|---|---|---|---|
| 3 | 2 | 4 | 1 |
| 4 | 3 | 1 | 2 |
| 2 | 1 | 3 | 4 |

**77**

| 3 | 4 | 2 | 1 |
|---|---|---|---|
| 1 | 2 | 3 | 4 |
| 4 | 3 | 1 | 2 |
| 2 | 1 | 4 | 3 |

**78**

| 1 | 2 | 4 | 3 |
|---|---|---|---|
| 3 | 4 | 2 | 1 |
| 4 | 1 | 3 | 2 |
| 2 | 3 | 1 | 4 |

Page 41

**79**

| 3 | 4 | 2 | 1 |
|---|---|---|---|
| 2 | 1 | 3 | 4 |
| 4 | 2 | 1 | 3 |
| 1 | 3 | 4 | 2 |

**80**

| 1 | 2 | 4 | 3 |
|---|---|---|---|
| 3 | 4 | 1 | 2 |
| 4 | 3 | 2 | 1 |
| 2 | 1 | 3 | 4 |

**81**

| 4 | 3 | 1 | 2 |
|---|---|---|---|
| 2 | 1 | 3 | 4 |
| 3 | 4 | 2 | 1 |
| 1 | 2 | 4 | 3 |

**82**

| 4 | 2 | 3 | 1 |
|---|---|---|---|
| 1 | 3 | 2 | 4 |
| 2 | 1 | 4 | 3 |
| 3 | 4 | 1 | 2 |

**83**

| 1 | 4 | 2 | 3 |
|---|---|---|---|
| 3 | 2 | 4 | 1 |
| 4 | 1 | 3 | 2 |
| 2 | 3 | 1 | 4 |

**84**

| 3 | 2 | 1 | 4 |
|---|---|---|---|
| 4 | 1 | 2 | 3 |
| 2 | 3 | 4 | 1 |
| 1 | 4 | 3 | 2 |

# Challenging

Page 42

**85**

| 4 | 3 | 2 | 1 |
|---|---|---|---|
| 2 | 1 | 3 | 4 |
| 3 | 4 | 1 | 2 |
| 1 | 2 | 4 | 3 |

**86**

| 4 | 2 | 1 | 3 |
|---|---|---|---|
| 1 | 3 | 2 | 4 |
| 3 | 1 | 4 | 2 |
| 2 | 4 | 3 | 1 |

**87**

| 2 | 3 | 4 | 1 |
|---|---|---|---|
| 1 | 4 | 3 | 2 |
| 4 | 1 | 2 | 3 |
| 3 | 2 | 1 | 4 |

**88**

| 4 | 1 | 3 | 2 |
|---|---|---|---|
| 3 | 2 | 4 | 1 |
| 2 | 3 | 1 | 4 |
| 1 | 4 | 2 | 3 |

**89**

| 4 | 2 | 3 | 1 |
|---|---|---|---|
| 3 | 1 | 2 | 4 |
| 1 | 3 | 4 | 2 |
| 2 | 4 | 1 | 3 |

**90**

| 4 | 1 | 3 | 2 |
|---|---|---|---|
| 3 | 2 | 1 | 4 |
| 1 | 4 | 2 | 3 |
| 2 | 3 | 4 | 1 |

Page 43

**91**

| 4 | 1 | 2 | 3 |
|---|---|---|---|
| 2 | 3 | 4 | 1 |
| 1 | 4 | 3 | 2 |
| 3 | 2 | 1 | 4 |

**92**

| 2 | 3 | 4 | 1 |
|---|---|---|---|
| 4 | 1 | 2 | 3 |
| 1 | 2 | 3 | 4 |
| 3 | 4 | 1 | 2 |

**93**

| 4 | 2 | 3 | 1 |
|---|---|---|---|
| 3 | 1 | 4 | 2 |
| 1 | 3 | 2 | 4 |
| 2 | 4 | 1 | 3 |

**94**

| 3 | 1 | 4 | 2 |
|---|---|---|---|
| 4 | 2 | 3 | 1 |
| 2 | 4 | 1 | 3 |
| 1 | 3 | 2 | 4 |

**95**

| 2 | 4 | 1 | 3 |
|---|---|---|---|
| 3 | 1 | 2 | 4 |
| 1 | 3 | 4 | 2 |
| 4 | 2 | 3 | 1 |

**96**

| 3 | 2 | 1 | 4 |
|---|---|---|---|
| 1 | 4 | 3 | 2 |
| 2 | 3 | 4 | 1 |
| 4 | 1 | 2 | 3 |

# Challenging

## Page 44

**97**

| 2 | 1 | 4 | 3 |
|---|---|---|---|
| 4 | 3 | 2 | 1 |
| 1 | 2 | 3 | 4 |
| 3 | 4 | 1 | 2 |

**98**

| 4 | 2 | 1 | 3 |
|---|---|---|---|
| 3 | 1 | 2 | 4 |
| 2 | 3 | 4 | 1 |
| 1 | 4 | 3 | 2 |

**99**

| 4 | 1 | 3 | 2 |
|---|---|---|---|
| 2 | 3 | 4 | 1 |
| 3 | 2 | 1 | 4 |
| 1 | 4 | 2 | 3 |

**100**

| 2 | 3 | 4 | 1 |
|---|---|---|---|
| 1 | 4 | 2 | 3 |
| 3 | 2 | 1 | 4 |
| 4 | 1 | 3 | 2 |

**101**

| 4 | 1 | 3 | 2 |
|---|---|---|---|
| 3 | 2 | 4 | 1 |
| 1 | 4 | 2 | 3 |
| 2 | 3 | 1 | 4 |

**102**

| 3 | 2 | 1 | 4 |
|---|---|---|---|
| 4 | 1 | 3 | 2 |
| 1 | 4 | 2 | 3 |
| 2 | 3 | 4 | 1 |

## Page 45

**103**

| 2 | 1 | 4 | 3 |
|---|---|---|---|
| 3 | 4 | 2 | 1 |
| 4 | 3 | 1 | 2 |
| 1 | 2 | 3 | 4 |

**104**

| 4 | 2 | 1 | 3 |
|---|---|---|---|
| 3 | 1 | 2 | 4 |
| 1 | 4 | 3 | 2 |
| 2 | 3 | 4 | 1 |

**105**

| 1 | 3 | 4 | 2 |
|---|---|---|---|
| 4 | 2 | 1 | 3 |
| 2 | 4 | 3 | 1 |
| 3 | 1 | 2 | 4 |

**106**

| 3 | 2 | 1 | 4 |
|---|---|---|---|
| 1 | 4 | 3 | 2 |
| 2 | 3 | 4 | 1 |
| 4 | 1 | 2 | 3 |

**107**

| 3 | 2 | 1 | 4 |
|---|---|---|---|
| 1 | 4 | 2 | 3 |
| 4 | 1 | 3 | 2 |
| 2 | 3 | 4 | 1 |

**108**

| 3 | 2 | 1 | 4 |
|---|---|---|---|
| 4 | 1 | 3 | 2 |
| 1 | 4 | 2 | 3 |
| 2 | 3 | 4 | 1 |

SUDOKIDS.com™

# Create Your Own

| | | | |
|---|---|---|---|
| | | | |
| | | | |
| | | | |
| | | | |

| | | | |
|---|---|---|---|
| | | | |
| | | | |
| | | | |
| | | | |

| | | | |
|---|---|---|---|
| | | | |
| | | | |
| | | | |
| | | | |

SUDOKIDS.com

| | | | |
|---|---|---|---|
| | | | |
| | | | |
| | | | |
| | | | |

| | | | |
|---|---|---|---|
| | | | |
| | | | |
| | | | |
| | | | |

| | | | |
|---|---|---|---|
| | | | |
| | | | |
| | | | |
| | | | |

# Sample Page

**Nail Biting**

No: 1237

| | | | | | | | | |
|---|---|---|---|---|---|---|---|---|
| 5 | | | | | | 8 | 6 | |
| | | | 1 | | 3 | | | |
| | 9 | | | | | | | |
| 7 | | | | | | | 4 | 3 |
| 8 | | 1 | | 5 | | | | |
| | | | | | | | | |
| | 4 | 3 | 9 | | | | | |
| | | | | 8 | | 5 | | |
| | | | | | | | | |

No: 1238

| | | | | | | | | |
|---|---|---|---|---|---|---|---|---|
| | | 6 | 5 | | | | 1 | 8 |
| | 3 | | | | | | | |
| | | | 7 | | | | | |
| 8 | | | | | | | | 7 |
| | | | | | 4 | 9 | | |
| | | | | 3 | | | | |
| | | | | 9 | | 4 | 3 | |
| 5 | | | 8 | | | | | |
| 7 | | | | | | | | |

No: 1239

| | | | | | | | | |
|---|---|---|---|---|---|---|---|---|
| | | | | 6 | | | | 4 |
| | 9 | | 5 | | | | | |
| | 3 | | | | | 8 | | |
| | | | 3 | | 8 | | 9 | |
| 6 | | | | | | 7 | | |
| 1 | | | | | 5 | | | |
| 7 | | | | 1 | | | | |
| | | | | | | | 3 | |
| | | | | | | 6 | | |

No: 1240

| | | | | | | | | |
|---|---|---|---|---|---|---|---|---|
| 8 | | | | 7 | | 4 | | |
| | 6 | | | | 3 | | | |
| | | | | | | | | |
| 5 | | | | | | | | 6 |
| 7 | | | | 4 | | | | |
| | | | 8 | | | | 9 | |
| | 9 | 3 | 6 | | | | | |
| | 1 | | | | | 2 | | |
| | | | | | | 7 | | |

No: 1241

| | | | | | | | | |
|---|---|---|---|---|---|---|---|---|
| | | 5 | 4 | | 8 | | | |
| | | | | | | | 3 | |
| | 8 | | | | | | | |
| 7 | | | 1 | 3 | | | | |
| 6 | | | | | | 8 | | |
| | | | | | | 9 | | |
| 3 | | | 7 | | | | 1 | |
| | | | | 6 | | 5 | | |
| | 9 | | | | | | | |

No: 1242

| | | | | | | | | |
|---|---|---|---|---|---|---|---|---|
| | | | 5 | 8 | | 2 | | |
| 6 | | | | | | 9 | | |
| | | 3 | | | | | | |
| 7 | | | 4 | | | | | |
| | 5 | | 2 | | | | | |
| | | | | | | | 6 | |
| | | | | 9 | 6 | | 3 | |
| 5 | 2 | | | | | | | |
| 1 | | | | | | | | |

Scaled down to fit page

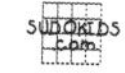

# Sudoku Puzzles for Kids.

## Ages 4-8

Thanks for trying our kids Sudoku puzzle book. Please visit www.sudokids.com for new titles, games, puzzles, country specific books, teacher resources, customization and bulk school ordering information.

www.sudokids.com



ISBN 978-0-620-40593-5

Made in the USA
Lexington, KY
25 March 2012